X GAMES

Moto X Freestyle

by Connie Colwell Miller

Reading Consultant:
Barbara J. Fox
Reading Specialist
North Carolina State University

Content Consultant:
Ben Hobson
Content Coordinator
Extreme Sports Channel
United Kingdom

Capstone press

Mankato, Minnesota

Blazers is published by Capstone Press,
151 Good Counsel Drive, P.O. Box 669, Mankato, Minnesota 56002.
www.capstonepress.com

Library of Congress Cataloging-in-Publication Data
Miller, Connie Colwell, 1976–
    Moto X freestyle / by Connie Colwell Miller.
    p. cm.—(Blazers. X games)
    Includes bibliographical references and index.
    ISBN-13: 978-1-4296-0107-8 (hardcover)
    ISBN-10: 1-4296-0107-8 (hardcover)
    1. Motocross—Juvenile literature. 2. ESPN X-Games—Juvenile literature.
I. Title. II. Series.
GV1060.12.M57 2008
796.7'56—dc22   2007001740

Summary: Describes the sport of freestyle motocross, focusing on the X Games,
including competitions and star athletes.

Essential content terms are bold and are defined at the bottom of the page where they first appear.

Editorial Credits
Mandy R. Robbins, editor; Bobbi J. Wyss, designer; Jo Miller, photo researcher

Photo Credits
AP/Wide World Photos/Ric Francis, 4–5
Corbis/Bo Bridges, 7, 8–9; Icon SMI/Shelly Castellano, 14–15; NewSport/
    Kohjiro Kinno, 16–17; NewSport/Steve Boyle, 6, 12, 18–19, 20–21, 22–23;
    Rueters/Henry Romero, 27
Dreamstime/Denis Pepin, 11; Stephen Coburn, 13
Getty Images Inc./Allsport/Darren England, 26; Lisa Blumenfeld, cover
iStockphoto/Randy Mayes, 28–29
ZUMA Press/Vaughn Youtz, 24–25

The publisher does not endorse products whose logos may appear on objects in
images in this book.

1 2 3 4 5 6 12 11 10 09 08 07

Table of Contents

One Amazing Run

On August 6, 2006, the
X Games rocked Los Angeles.
Freestyle motocross (FMX) fans
cheered as Travis Pastrana attacked
the **course**.

course (KORSS)—a set path; FMX riders compete
on courses with obstacles, jumps, and turns.

Pastrana cruised up ramps
and busted a few flashy tricks. Then
Pastrana did an upside-down lazyboy.
He laid flat on his motorcycle while
flipping the bike.

When Pastrana finished his **run**, fans screamed. It was clear he had earned the gold medal.

run (RUHN)—a timed series of motocross tricks during which competitors try to impress the judges

Pastrana won his first gold medal at age 15.

FMX Basics

In FMX events, daredevil riders soar over huge jumps on their dirt bikes. Riders do stunts while flying through the air.

Superman
seat grab

Stunts have names like the cliff hanger, Superman seat grab, and can can. In the cliff hanger, the bike drops out from under the rider. He catches the handlebars on top of his feet!

BLAZER FACT

There are gaps of 60 to 90 feet (18 to 27 meters) between jumps.

cliff hanger

BLAZER FACT

When performing a rock solid, riders let go of their motorcycles completely!

To do a can can, FMX riders swing their bodies around the bike. Daring riders do other tricks while flipping their bikes over.

Exciting Events

In the X Games, FMX riders challenge each other in **heats**. Riders have two minutes to prove their skill in each heat.

heat (HEET)—one of several FMX runs that determines who advances in the competition

Winners of the first heats go head to head in the main event. Judges rate each run with a score from zero to 100.

BLAZER FACT

FMX got its start from the crazy tricks motocross riders did at the end of races.

FMX riders score points for high jumps and difficult tricks. They get more points for moving smoothly from one trick to the next.

FMX Course Diagram

jumps

jumps

launch ramp

FMX Greats

At age 17, Mike Metzger was already **inventing** tricks like the switchblade. To do this trick, Metzger kicks his feet to the left. Then he twists his body around.

invent (in-VENT)—to create something new

Carey Hart is another FMX star.
Hart invented the Hart attack. During
this trick, riders do a handstand on
their bike while soaring through the air.

FMX stars like Pastrana, Hart, and Metzger blaze the way for new riders. The future of FMX is sure to include crazy new stunts that will thrill fans.

lazyboy

Flying Freestyle!

Glossary

course (KORSS)—a set path; FMX riders compete on courses with obstacles, jumps, and turns.

heat (HEET)—one of several early runs that determine which riders advance to the main event

invent (in-VENT)—to create a new thing or method

rate (RAYT)—to judge the quality or worth of something

run (RUHN)—a rider's turn on the course

Read More

Doeden, Matt. *Motocross Freestyle.* To the Extreme. Mankato, Minn.: Capstone Press, 2005.

Savage, Jeff. *Travis Pastrana.* Amazing Athletes. Minneapolis: Lerner, 2006.

Schwartz, Tina. *Motocross Freestyle.* Dirt Bikes. Mankato, Minn.: Capstone Press, 2004.

Internet Sites

FactHound offers a safe, fun way to find Internet sites related to this book. All of the sites on FactHound have been researched by our staff.

Here's how:
1. Visit *www.facthound.com*
2. Choose your grade level.
3. Type in this special code **1429601078** for age-appropriate sites. You may also browse subjects by clicking on letters, or by clicking on pictures or words.
4. Click on the **Fetch It** button.

FactHound will fetch the best sites for you!

Index